LIVING IN THE SHADOW OF THE GHOSTS OF GRIEF

Also by Dr. Alan Wolfelt

Companioning the Bereaved:
A Soulful Guide for Caregivers

Healing Your Grieving Heart: 100 Practical Ideas

Healing Your Grieving Heart for Kids: 100 Practical Ideas

Healing Your Grieving Heart for Teens: 100 Practical Ideas

The Journey Through Grief: Reflections on Healing

Understanding Your Grief: Ten Essential Touchstones
for Finding Hope and Healing Your Heart

The Understanding Your Grief Journal:
Exploring the Ten Essential Touchstones

When Your Pet Dies: A Guide to
Mourning, Remembering and Healing

LIVING IN THE SHADOW OF THE GHOSTS OF GRIEF

Step into the Light

Alan D. Wolfelt, Ph.D.

Companion
PRESS

Companion Press is an imprint of the
Center for Loss and Life Transition
3735 Broken Bow Road
Fort Collins, Colorado 80526
970-226-6050
www.centerforloss.com

Companion Press books may be purchased in bulk for sales promotions, premiums or fundraisers. Please contact the publisher at the above address for more information.

Printed in the United States of America

20 19 18 17 16 15   5 4 3 2

ISBN 978-1-879651-51-7

*To my most important teachers:
Megan, Christopher and Jaimie Wolfelt. These
three precious children are constant reminders to
me of the importance of unconditional love and
of all that is soulful in the world around me.*

Companion Press is dedicated to the education and support of both the bereaved and bereavement caregivers.

We believe that those who companion the bereaved by walking with them as they journey in grief have a wondrous opportunity: to help others embrace and grow through grief—and to lead fuller, more deeply-lived lives themselves because of this important ministry.

Companion
PRESS

For a complete catalog and ordering information, write or call:

Companion Press
The Center for Loss and Life Transition
3735 Broken Bow Road
Fort Collins, CO 80526
(970) 226-6050
www.centerforloss.com

Contents

Preface

When you suffer a loss of any kind, you normally and naturally grieve inside. To heal your grief, you must express it. That is, you must mourn your grief. If you don't, you will carry your grief into your future, and it will undermine your happiness for the rest of your life. The good news is that with commitment and the help of a compassionate companion, you can heal your carried grief and go on to live a life of joy. These are the fundamental principles of this book.

As I travel North America teaching about the need to mourn well so you can live well, I have met thousands of grievers who have taught me, in return, that they carry longstanding and cumulative grief, often stemming from their childhood. They are able to see, as together we explore the need to mourn, that their carried grief may be causing a host of problems in their current lives. I began to call this phenomenon "living in the shadow of the ghosts of grief." Many of my books help grievers tap into their natural capacity to mourn a recent death. This book helps grievers acknowledge and mourn losses and deaths that may have occurred long ago. Its goal is to help grievers heal old wounds so they can finally love and live fully.

Thank you for taking the time and energy to reflect on the words that make up this book. I wish you well on your personal journey of helping yourself and others heal from life losses. May this book offer you something for your head, your heart, and your spirit. If you find this book helpful, consider dropping me a note about your journey and allow me to learn from you about how you have been touched by the losses that shape all of our lives.

I am also grateful to the thousands of people who have participated in my retreat learning experiences about grief and who have embraced the "compassionate companioning" philosophy I hold so dear. Most important, I thank those who have gone before me for teaching me that grief is a birthright of life and that giving and receiving love is the essence of having meaning and purpose in our lives.

Alan D. Wolfelt

Introduction

*"Your pain is the breaking of the shell
that encloses your understanding."*
— Kahlil Gibran

A central truth is that all of us as human beings are connected in our experiences of loss and grief. If you have picked up this book and are reading these words, you are probably consciously aware that you have been impacted by life losses. Each and every one of our lives involves natural transitions, unwanted endings and new beginnings.

Yet, perhaps you have noticed that many people in our culture seem to avoid embracing life losses and try to go around them instead of through them. This book, directed from my heart to your heart, is an invitation to go to that spiritual place inside you that is aching to find "safe places" and "safe people" with whom you can openly acknowledge the griefs influencing your life. In part, my hope is that this book will help you understand if and why you are living in the shadow of the ghosts of grief so that you can step into the light.

For you see, as I continue to grow and learn, I have come to believe that it is in embracing our carried grief that we find relief from our life problems (e.g., anxieties, depressions, addictive behaviors, difficulties with giving and receiving love). I passionately believe that when we don't authentically mourn life losses, we can't live or love well. My observation is that many North Americans have come to believe that grief is an enemy to be fought instead of an experience to be embraced and befriended. Yet, it is the befriending process that contains the beginnings of grace.

> **Grace:** The knowing that you are not alone,
> that you are always accompanied.
> Grace expands your will by giving you
> a courage you did not have before.
> Grace invites you to befriend your
> grief and mourn your life losses.

I invite you to consider that to inhibit, delay, convert or avoid grief is to condemn yourself to a living death. Living fully requires that you feel fully. It means being completely one with what you are experiencing. If you are unwilling or unable to give attention to how loss and grief shape your life path, you will project your symptoms into your body, your relationships and your worldview. Any unhealed grief will linger, influencing all aspects of your life, your living, and particularly, your loving.

How ironic is it that we try to push away or fend off what is a life-given condition—the need to mourn? Some families have a long-held tradition of responding defensively in the face of life losses. For many, the resistance to the pain and discomfort that accompanies loss is passed down generationally. When family rules do not allow for true feelings, the capacity to mourn is inhibited, delayed, converted, or avoided completely. The family rule, although unwritten and usually unspoken, is often loud and clear: "Thou shall not mourn!" Yet, until you can authentically mourn life losses, you become "stuck" and are at risk for depression, anxiety and a host of other problems.

The Shadow of the Ghosts

Grief is a natural and necessary response to the many losses we encounter in our life journeys. Many of the losses we experience are little, while some are big and some gigantic. Some are excruciatingly painful while others cause us to feel barely a twinge.

If you have gone through life expressing your painful feelings of loss—big and little, excruciating and barely-there, you're probably not living in the shadow of the ghosts of grief. If, on the other hand, you're like most of us grief-swallowers and loss-deniers, you may well be.

When you live in the shadow of the ghosts of grief, you suffer, often unknowingly, from unacknowledged and unexpressed feelings of loss. These stuffed feelings are often longstanding, stemming from your childhood and young adulthood. You may have many ghosts—that is, many unacknowledged losses, or you may find that your ghost is identifiably singular—a specific loss that devastated you, even if you didn't realize it at the time.

This book is about my observation that many people are living in the shadow of the ghosts of grief. The person living in the shadow often has symptoms that suggest that the pain of grief has been inhibited, delayed, converted or avoided altogether. However, what I'll go on to describe as fall-out symptoms stay present, driving the person's life, trying to get the attention they deserve.

I also use the term "carried grief" to describe unacknowledged and unmourned grief. When you experience loss but you do not mourn the normal and necessary resulting feelings of grief, you "carry" that grief forward into your future. This carried grief results in a muting of one's spirit, or divine spark, or what Meister Eckhart described as "that which gives depth and purpose to our living." And, when the spirit is muted, there is an ongoing hampering of your ability to live your life with meaning and purpose.

Many of us have been taught that pain is an indication that something is wrong, and that we should quickly find ways to alleviate our pain. In our culture, pain and feelings of loss are experiences most people try to avoid. We often have no clue as to what to do with our pain other than to deny or self-treat it. Why? Because the role of pain and suffering is misunderstood. Normal thoughts and feelings after a loss are often seen as unnecessary and inappropriate. All too often we have been taught to "keep busy, carry on, keep our chins up, and get over it." The unfortunate result is that we carry our pain and go on to live in the shadow of the ghosts of our grief.

Yes, our carried pain will keep trying to get our attention until we discover the courage to gently, and in small doses, open to its presence. The alternative—denying or suppressing our pain—is in fact more painful.

While it us true that carried pain from death loss often causes us to live in the shadow of the ghosts of grief, I urge you to remember that many of us carry pain from a multitude of life losses. Any and all life losses, if unmourned, may result in the carried pain that stultifies lives. So, as you read the chapters that follow, consider not only the deaths of those you were close to but also all other types of losses that may have affected your life.

The darkness of the shadow in which you live may be seeping into all aspects of your life. Part Three of this book will help you identify whether or not you may be living in the shadow of the ghosts of grief. Part Four will help you understand and work towards mourning your carried grief so that you can step out of the shadow and into the full light of life.

If you find this book helpful, please consider writing me about your experiences. In doing so, you will allow me to learn from you and encourage me to continue to attempt to create "safe places" and "safe people" where people can discover the courage to authentically mourn.

Part One

Change means loss; loss means
grief;
grief requires mourning

"Loss is an integral part of human existence, a fact which has profound consequences from birth to death."
— David Peretz

From the moment we are conceived, our lives are a series of transitions.

We slide from the dark, cozy womb into the bright, cold, colossal world—a shocking transition indeed! We nurse at the breast then are weaned. We learn to walk and talk. We attach to our parents then are forced to detach from them when we are placed in daycare or school. We learn to ride a bike and swim. Our baby teeth fall out. We make friends and lose them. Brothers and sisters may be born. Our parents may divorce. Someone we love may die.

As we grow to adulthood, many of the normal and natural life transitions we experience are joyful. Some are painful. Most are both. We learn that change—for good or for worse—can be difficult. This is because change is almost always part loss, part gain. When we move to a new neighborhood, we may lose old friends and gain new ones. When we leave home to go to school or start a life of our own, we may thrill at the newfound independence but grieve the loss of day-to-day nurturing from our family.

Along life's journey, there are repeated losses—of security, of connectedness, of innocence. We also learn that some forms of change feel like pure loss. A pet dies. A best friend moves away. A boyfriend or girlfriend decides they no longer love us. And one day, a person we love dies. We learn very early that it feels good to love, but it hurts deeply when love is lost. We learn that loss and grief are inevitable parts of our humanness. Grief is the price we pay for our capacity to give and receive love.

So from the time we are little, we feel grief. And when we are little, we express both our joy and our grief. We laugh and giggle. We cry and throw tantrums. We know instinctively that transitions often stir up strong feelings, but as we grow older, our culture teaches us to downplay the "bad" strong feelings and emphasize the "good" ones. It's OK to laugh and giggle when we are feeling happy, but it's not so OK to cry and throw tantrums when we are feeling scared, anxious, angry and sad.

By the time we're adults, we're often so trained to ignore or deny our feelings of grief and loss that we can hardly identify when we're feeling bad or, especially, why we're feeling bad. Grief is so much more a part of our lives than many of us realize or care to acknowledge.

The Difference Between Grief and Mourning

"There is no love without loss. And there is no moving beyond loss without some experiences of mourning. To be unable to mourn is to be unable to enter into the great human lifecycle of death and rebirth—to be unable, that is, to live again."
— Eric Lifton

So we grieve when we experience a transition or loss. That is, we feel painful feelings inside us. The word *grief* means the constellation of internal thoughts and feelings you experience within you about a loss. Think of grief as the container. It holds all of your thoughts, feelings, and images of your experience when you have a loss.

The word *mourning*, on the other hand, means something different. Mourning is when you take the grief you have on the inside and express it outside of yourself. Mourning is "grief gone public" or "the outward expression of grief." When you cry, you're mourning. When you talk to someone about your painful thoughts and feelings, you're mourning. When you write about your grief in a journal, you're mourning.

You can mourn in physical, emotional, cognitive, social and spiritual ways. You can jog out your grief; you can paint it; you can pray it. Anything you do to express your grief counts as mourning.

I believe that to heal your grief, you must mourn it. A basic premise of this book is that to give and receive love well—and to simply live well—we must mourn well. By "mourning well," I mean openly and honestly expressing our thoughts and feelings from the inside to the outside—no pretense, no repression, no inhibitions. The losses we encounter demand our attention as we work (oh yes, it is work!) to integrate them into our lives. Somewhere, in the collision between heart, which searches for permanency and connection, and brain, which acknowledges separation and loss, there is a need for all of us to mourn.

Self-love is a prerequisite to expressive love (i.e., loving outside of self; opening oneself to others). The essence of self-love is to be true to ones feelings and needs when we are mourning. Authentic love can only take place if we don't cut ourselves off from the need to mourn, and, instead of running from our grief, we have the courage to befriend the pain of loss.

Courage originates from the Old French word for heart (*coeur*). Your courage grows for those things in life that impact you deeply. Our life losses invite our hearts to open. An open heart is a "well of reception;" it is moved entirely by what it has experienced. We often get encouraged to close our hearts to our grief. Yet I am convinced that the pain that surrounds the closed heart is the pain of living against ourselves, the pain of denying how loss changes us, and the pain of feeling alone and isolated—unable to mourn, unable to love and be loved by those around us.

Instead of dying while we are alive, we can choose to remain open to our pain. If instead we deny our pain, we also unknowingly defend against all that brings meaning and purpose to life, leaving us feeling alone and isolated—cut off from our own humanity.

An ancient Hebrew sage once observed, "If you want life, you must expect suffering." Paradoxically, it is gathering the courage to move toward our pain that ultimately leads to the healing of our wounded hearts. Our integrity is engaged by our feelings and the commitment to honor the truth in them.

In part, helping yourself authentically mourn is to have the discipline to face the work of mourning. The word discipline means "being a disciple unto oneself." When you are able to be a disciple unto yourself, you are honoring your own rhythm and the intuitive ebbs and flows of grief.

Befriending Your Grief

> *"To suppress the grief, the pain, is to condemn oneself to a living death. Living fully means feeling fully; it means being completely one with what you are experiencing and not holding it at arm's length."*
> — Phillip Kapleau

Refusal to descend into our life sorrows can destroy much of our capacity to enjoy life, living and loving. After all, how can we relate to ourselves or others if we don't feel? Moving away from grief results in moving away from ourselves and other people. The epidemic of grief avoidance we now witness as a culture gets in the way of our capacity to be transformed by our pain, our sorrow and our suffering.

To befriend the pain of our life losses is to acknowledge we cannot go around it, we must go through it. In our willingness to gently embrace the pain of our losses, we are in effect honoring our pain and freeing ourselves to live fully until we die.

"What?", you naturally protest, "honor the pain?" Crazy as it may sound, our pain is the key that opens our hearts and ushers us into our healing.

First, I want to acknowledge that when we initially experience loss, it is instinctive, normal and necessary to want to push away or avoid raw emotions—temporarily.

There is a delicate balance between the normal need for evasion of the reality of the loss and the necessary encountering of the reality of the loss. The path of the heart of grief is paradoxical. It moves, often simultaneously, toward both evasion and encounter. Spiritual maturity in grief is the capacity to inhabit the paradox, to embrace both the instinct to avoid and the need to encounter,

to both push away and surrender to grief
and sorrow.

So yes, temporarily seeking to avoid or deny the
pain of grief is normal and necessary. It helps
us survive, at first, what would otherwise be
unsurvivable. And even when we begin to embrace
the pain of our grief, it is normal and necessary to
move back and forth between embracing the pain
and distancing ourselves from it. The pain that
results from significant life losses is too much to
bear all at once. So, we "dose" ourselves with our
pain a little at a time. It is when our patterns of
avoidance and denial dominate and become rigid
and fixed in place that we are at risk for living in
the shadow of the ghosts of grief.

DOSING GRIEF
The concept of dosing our grief recognizes
that we cannot embrace the pain of
grief all at once out of some ill-founded
need to "overcome" it. Instead, we must
allow ourselves to "dose" the pain—feel
it in small waves then allow it to retreat
until we are ready for the next wave.

Trying to stay in control by denying, inhibiting or converting grief can result in what Kierkegaard termed "unconscious despair." Doing the soul work of grief demands going through suffering and integrating it in ways that help unite you with your fellow strugglers and the greater community of people.

The very essence of this book is to help you honor your pain on the pathway to living your life with meaning and purpose. Honoring means "recognizing the value of and respecting." I realize that when we live in a mourning-avoidant culture it is not natural to see grief as something to honor. Yet, the capacity to love requires the necessity to mourn. To honor our grief is not self-destructive or harmful, it is self-sustaining and life-giving.

My hope is that you will gently befriend your own losses and griefs as you explore what follows. Trying to shield ourselves from the grief that touches our lives only results in shielding us from all that we love, leaving us feeling alone, isolated, depressed, and anxious.

In reality, what is not faced within and eventually mourned is still carried as a deep personal pain. To experience healing and eventually to contribute healing to others and the world around us, we are summoned to the wilderness as we encounter life's journey. Where we do not go willingly, sooner or later we may be dragged.

The good news is that we as humans come equipped with an organic capacity to integrate our life transitions, losses and endings. Yet, when you live in a mourning-avoidant culture where grief is supposed to be "overcome," "let go of" and "resolved," it can be difficult, at times impossible, to remember and celebrate that we can mourn.

The fact that we are capable of grieving and mourning reminds us that we are meant to embrace losses and integrate them into our lives. Until we get contaminated to deny our feelings of loss, we instinctively feel sadness, hurt, pain and fear when loss occurs. The expression of these and many other potential feelings is what helps us heal our griefs.

"Grief work" and "active mourning" is the very pathway through which you reconcile your losses. It is up to each one of us to allow and gently embrace the mourning that all of life's conditions require. It is up to us to learn to trust that in befriending our grief, we enhance the quality of our lives. In reading this book you are accepting the invitation to engage in living fully until you die.

In reading this book, you are, in part, acknowledging a need to surrender to the reality of your life losses. I believe that surrendering to your losses and realizing you can't control them give birth to your self-compassion and grace. The grief that touches our lives has its own voice and should not be compromised by our need for comparison, judgment, or control.

The opposite of befriending your life losses is to try to control them. Underneath the impulse to control is fear that you will have to experience feelings of helplessness and hurt. Befriending leads to integration of loss into your life; control leads to refusal to surrender and the evolution of "shadow of the ghosts" symptoms. In large part, the choice to surrender is yours and yours alone.

To surrender acknowledges you cannot insulate yourself from loss, grief and the need to mourn. The need to control often comes about because you have been taught to make grief your enemy instead of your friend. You try to control because you have learned to fear grief. You have grown up in a culture that attempts to "overcome" grief as opposed to experiencing it. It hurts to allow feelings of sadness into our life. It hurts to let yourself know what you have lost.

The need to control has become such an unconscious part of North American culture that many people think they can let go of control by simply deciding to. Yet, we don't let go of control and surrender to our grief; we let go of the belief that we have control and surrender to our grief. If we stay in control, we miss the invitation to humility and self-compassion.

My sense is that you the reader would not be giving attention to this book if you didn't recognize the important need to embrace your life losses. I do hope this book will inspire a larger discussion about our mourning-avoidant culture, eventually leading to more dialogue about our cultural unwillingness to befriend our grief and be humble and self-compassionate.

While grief is a powerful experience, so too is your capacity to help in your own healing. You wouldn't be reading this book if you were not interested in helping yourself or your fellow human beings mourn life losses. So, savor this book, underline what speaks to you, create a reflective journal to help wrap words around your experiences, and most importantly, do not hesitate to reach out and find what I will describe as a "compassionate companion" to help you mourn your carried pain and step out of the shadow of the ghosts of grief and into the light.

Part Two

Why we carry grief instead of mourning it

"If you bring forth what is within you, what you bring forth will save you. If you do not bring forth what is within you, what you do not bring forth will destroy you."
— Acts of John, Gnostic Scripture

We've learned that we pack up all our unmourned grief and carry it into our future. And I've mentioned that our society is good at inviting us to deny and repress our pain, which causes us to carry our grief forward instead of mourning it as we encounter it.

But why, if we're born knowing how to express our grief, do most of us learn to repress or deny it?

There are a number of factors, some that have been predominant in Western culture for millennia and some that have converged only in recent decades, that inhibit authentic mourning in our culture. Allow me to explore a few with you:

Family-of-Origin Modeling

Each of us brings our personal history of our child and teen years into our adult lives. Our parents and other significant adults are the most influential models we have for how to experience and navigate the world. What our parents did or didn't do with their own grief and loss experiences has a great impact on how we experience and express—or don't express—a multitude of emotions. Legacies of grief and loss will find expression down through the generations. As previously acknowledged, some family rules surrounding loss are loud and clear: "Thou shall not mourn."

Some families pass down a longstanding style of responding defensively in the face of loss. For many, the resistance to mourn openly and honestly is passed down generationally. Obviously, where family rules do not allow for true feelings, the natural capacity to mourn becomes thwarted, often resulting in carried grief and living in the shadow of the ghosts of grief.

Imagine a child who experiences a loss and is responded to with support, empathy, and unconditional love. This child's right to mourn is affirmed, and she learns to respond to her life experiences, both happy and sad, with the natural responses that her psyche conjures. She will grow up being able to know, express, and normalize her feelings, internalizing the capacity to have empathy for herself and others.

As life unfolds, she will still come to have losses and additional challenges; however, with this modeling of the importance of befriending her feelings and expressing them openly and honestly, she is able to integrate losses into her life with her sense of "self" intact. She has been blessed by growing up in what we call an "open-family system" surrounding loss and grief.

By contrast, imagine a child who experiences a loss and is denied the opportunity to identify and experience her feelings because the adults around her don't recognize this need. Instead of learning about the need to mourn, she has to create defenses to prevent her awareness of these feelings. For example, she may learn to project or displace feelings onto others, or internalize these feelings, resulting in low self-esteem and preventing her from finding deeper fulfillment and real intimacy in her life. She is living in what we call a "closed-family system" surrounding loss and grief.

While the loss this second child experiences is the source of her initial wound, the even greater and longer-lasting wound is caused by the lack of the opportunity or support to authentically mourn the grief of the initial wound. Sometimes her unacknowledged feelings express themselves as irritability, chronic anxiety, low-grade depression, and, in general, a negative outlook on life. The defensive barriers she learns to create put her at risk for fall-out symptoms such as depression, anxiety, difficulty with intimate relationships, addictive behaviors and other problems discussed in Part Three of this book.

The Grief-Avoidance Wounding Process

Often, children and teens who live in a closed-family system surrounding loss and grief issues experience the following wounding process, which affects the rest of their lives:

1. They experience a loss without parental or family recognition of their special needs to grieve and mourn.

2. They experience a lack of opportunity to integrate the resulting pain, hurt and suffering. (They grieve inside but are not allowed or encouraged to mourn.)

3. They then protect themselves from repeated injury from future losses by creating defense mechanisms.

4. They minimize, deny or disconnect from the significance of "carried grief."

5. They end up living in the shadow of the ghosts of grief.

If you recognize that this wounding process may have occurred in your childhood or adolescence, you will probably discover that your fall-out symptoms of carried grief will keep trying to get your attention until you give them the attention they deserve.

Fear of Painful Emotions

"Only when we are no longer
afraid do we begin to live."
— Dorothy Thompson

The opposite of embracing pain and allowing ourselves to mourn is control. As I explained in Part One, underneath the controlling impulse is fear: the fear that we will experience feelings that are painful. As grief enters into our lives, many of us have been taught that giving these feelings too much attention is a sign of weakness or breakdown. In fact, many people try to head off losses in the first place by controlling. After all, you don't have to grieve and mourn if everything comes out your way. I believe we control because we are afraid of emotions that grief brings into our lives.

In addition, the emotions of grief are often referred to as "negative," as if they are inherently bad emotions to experience. This judgment feeds our culture's attitude that these emotions should be denied or overcome. We think we can resolve grief instead of coming to understand that we integrate grief into our lives and are forever transformed by it. In reality, the care-eliciting emotions of grief are what alerts compassionate companions that we have special needs that call for support and comfort.

Self-Interest Before Community Interest

"I am a part of all that I have met."
— Alfred Tennyson

Many people grieve but don't mourn because of a preoccupation with self to the exclusion of community. "You can't depend on anybody else." "You've got to look out for Number One." So the sayings go. Well, it appears many North Americans have taken these clichés to the extreme.

For some, the goals of self-suffering and self-determination are the principal centerpieces of self-development. We are encouraged to think of ourselves as individual centers of consciousness, with the capacity for logical analysis. Therefore, some logically reason, "There is no point in experiencing feelings. After all, it won't bring back what I have lost."

As we use our heads, we seem to be forgetting our hearts as well as our need for community. Self-preoccupation results in more grieving and less mourning of life losses. "Doing it on one's own" is counter to the need for a shared, expressive response to loss.

For example, funeral ceremonies are intended to activate support systems among one's family, friends and the greater community. The trends toward private ceremonies and even the elimination of funerals altogether reflect in part our placement of self-interest before community interest. (Another main function of ceremony is to encourage emotional expression, so when we choose not to have a funeral or memorial ceremony, we're choosing to move into the shadow.)

Bad Theology

"Faith is more basic than language or theology."
— Sydney Carter

While many faith communities lovingly support people who are hurting and experiencing the pain of life losses, some do not. There is a body of thought that judges those who struggle emotionally as being "in sin." They are not "obedient" or "don't have enough faith," or, as I heard someone say recently, "They don't spend enough time reading the Bible."

Faced with this kind of judgment, people experiencing painful feelings of loss sometimes learn to pretend they are doing better than they really are, or leave their faith community because it does not provide a safe harbor for their feelings of loss and grief. Again, while many faith groups understand and support the truth of "Blessed are those who mourn," some do not, and members end up turning away from their faith communities at a time of critical need.

This kind of bad theology often sends the hurting person into isolation and hiding. And when you hide, you end up grieving, not mourning. You will recall that, by definition, mourning means "a shared response to loss." In the face of judgment surrounding feelings of loss, many people shut down and begin to live in the shadow of the ghosts of grief.

Compare the griever's conditional, judgmental place of worship with an unconditional, loving grief support-group experience. Through the lens of bad theology, it is often unacceptable to experience emotional and spiritual distress. However, in a loving, grace-filled support group, it is expected that people experience distress. In the former experience, people often project looking good and feeling good but actually get worse, and in the latter, they look bad and feel bad, but slowly get better because they learn to integrate the pain into their lives.

The Psychopharmacology Revolution

"It seemed like this was one big Prozac nation, one big mess of malaise."
— Elizabeth Wurtzel

The emotional and spiritual pain of grief has become perceived by many as a disorder that should be "treated" by outside experts—if not by some form of counseling then by some form of medication that alters the emotions you are experiencing. In medical science, the all-too-common treatment plan says: If there is pain and hurt that result in symptoms, medicate as soon as possible.

I submit that the pharmaceutical response to depression has been both a blessing and a curse. While helping people with severe, chronic and disabling conditions, the use of antidepressants has also resulted in a tendency to equate the absence of symptoms of pain and suffering with "good mental health." What we used to call melancholy, despair, or normal misery that life sometimes brings into our paths, we now quickly refer to as clinical depression—a biochemical disorder that should be treated with brain-altering chemicals.

This trend of medicating away difficult yet normal human emotions has made it nearly impossible for people to see value in befriending the emotions of grief. When we reflect on pain and suffering in contemporary times, all too many people think of pathology and treatment, not the normalcy and necessity of the full range of human emotions.

I have always enjoyed the old maxim that says, "The longest distance between any two points is the shortest." In immediately turning to medication management when painful feelings arise, we reflect our tendency to panic in the face of grief. By taking the short route, we at times end up taking longer than we would have if we had taken the longer route to begin with. The work of mourning simply takes time and attention—often a long time and a lot of attention. But this time and attention is the only true path to healing grief; medicating it away sometimes makes the underlying problem worse.

Contemporary Mental Health Care's
Focus on Efficiency Versus Effectiveness

"We may define therapy as a search for value."
— Abraham Maslow

For those people who do seek help with feelings of loss and grief, the sad reality is that they enter a care system that is currently confusing efficiency with effectiveness. Our present emphasis on managed care is appropriately titled in that caregivers are taught that their role is to "manage" or "resolve" grief as quickly as possible.

While some would like to think humans can quickly and efficiently overcome grief, reality suggests otherwise. This short-term focus on mental health care and the popularity of brief, solution-oriented therapies implies a rational and mechanistic understanding of what is actually a spiritual journey involving the heart and soul.

Quick fixes may in fact achieve temporary repression of normal symptoms of grief. But, we must ask ourselves, at what price? Repressed feelings always return to haunt the human psyche. If we try to resist the overwhelming power of grief, it will inevitably express itself through fall-out consequences such as difficulty in intimate relationships, addictive behaviors, and chronic depression.

This current approach to mental health care is actually contributing to an epidemic of carried grief in North America. Rather than allowing for the creation of safe places to mourn and acknowledging the need to slow down, not speed up, this current model encourages people to reach efficient "closure" on any and all feelings. Pain and feelings of loss are seen as unnecessary and inappropriate. Yet, only in having the safety of people and places where we can move toward our wounds do we ultimately integrate our life losses.

This current philosophy actually reinforces destructive social messages such as, "Carry on," "Keep your chin up" and "Keep busy." It's as if our current model of care shields its very self from acknowledging human pain and loss, while not providing places for people to mourn. Managed care has placed the focus on short-term, overt, measurable "progress" in grief. It's as if getting the person back to work is more important than restoring the soul. The human heart doesn't heal according to a time-clock; when it comes to embracing grief, faster is not better.

A "Constant State of Urgency" Negates the Capacity to Feel

"Beware the barrenness of a busy life."
— Socrates

The culture we live in seems to instill within us what I have termed a "constant state of urgency." We must always be going places and doing things. Interestingly enough, a common piece of trite advice given to many of us when we experience loss is, "Keep really busy."

The faster we go personally and as a society, the less we are available to experience loss-related feelings. Many people believe the antidote to sadness is urgency and speed. The paradox is that the faster you go, the more you move away from integrating loss into your life.

Inability to be in Liminal Space

"Anxiety is the space between the
'now' and the 'then.'"
— Richard Abell

In other books I have written about grief, I have used the metaphor of the wilderness to describe the journey that is grief. Think of grief as a wilderness— a vast, inhospitable forest. The surroundings are unfamiliar and often brutal. The griever is cold and tired. Yet, she must journey through the wilderness and learn to follow the sometimes hard-to-follow trail that leads to healing.

Being in the middle of the wilderness of grief is like being in the middle of nowhere. The griever often feels lost, alone, disoriented and confused. The concept of "liminal space" is another way to describe this feeling. *Limina* is the Latin word for threshold, the space betwixt and between. Liminal space is that spiritual place we hate to be, but where the experience of grief leads us.

We don't like pain, sadness, anxiety, ambiguity, loss of control—all normal symptoms in the wilderness of grief. The challenge for the griever is to allow himself to be in this liminal space without rushing himself to "resolve" or "get over" his grief. Sadly, our culture teaches us to be so intolerant of liminal situations that we often find a shortcut out as soon as possible—and so pick up our grief and begin to carry it.

This chapter has explored some of the factors that invite us to shut down to life losses. What others can you think of? The repercussions of this shutting down are that many people in our culture are grieving but not mourning. They are carrying their pain and living in the shadow of the ghosts of grief. And they are having the sorts of emotional and spiritual problems described in Part Three, next, as a result.

As you read about the fall-out symptoms of carried grief, however, be hopeful. Keep in mind that you can move out from the shadow of the ghosts of grief and step into the light. Parts Four and Five of this book will help you do just that.

Part Three

Are you carrying grief?

*"The frightening thing about loss is
what we do to ourselves to avoid it.
We know we cannot live without
losing, but this knowledge does not
prevent us from seeking to protect
ourselves. So we narrow our souls.
We draw ourselves tighter and tighter.
No longer open to the world with all
its hurts, we feel safe. By narrowing
ourselves, though, we end up with
more hurt than if we were free."*
— David Wolpe

When you carry your pain from life losses instead
of mourning that pain, it will come back to haunt
you. It will keep trying to get your attention until
you give it the attention it demands and deserves.
As Michel de Montaigne once observed, "The
man who fears suffering is already suffering from
what he fears."

If your pain is left unhealed, it destroys your
enthusiasm for life and living. It can deny you
your creativity, your gifts, your talents. The result

is that these parts of yourself go stagnant or unclaimed inside of you, wishing they could get out but feeling trapped.

It is as if you have an imaginary cage surrounding you. In the cage are a multitude of potential symptoms reflecting that you are carrying the pain of grief. Trapped inside the cage, you are devoid of the desire to fulfill your life dreams, which is the very essence of creating a meaningful life and fulfilling your spiritual potential.

Fall-Out Symptoms of Carried Grief

Following are some of the common fall-out symptoms I have observed in people who carry the pains of life grief and have not had the opportunity to authentically mourn. A culture that too often labels these kinds of symptoms as pathology, that shames people for openly mourning life losses, a culture preoccupied with quick fixes for emotional pain, invariably ends up inviting people to carry grief. So I ask you not to further shame yourself if you recognize some of the following symptoms in yourself.

Now let's explore some of the potential fall-out symptoms that may be entrapping your soul, forcing you to carry out an ever-reflexive response to life that grounds you not in the present, but in the past. Later in the chapter I will present another way of thinking of the symptoms of carried grief that I call "grief avoidance response styles." You may find aspects of yourself in both the fall-out symptoms and the grief avoidance response styles—or more in one than the other. You may also notice that there is overlap between the two ways of thinking about carried grief symptoms. The point here is to consider your current ways of being in the world and how those ways may have been caused by carried grief.

Fall-Out Symptoms of Carried Grief
- Difficulties with trust and intimacy
- Depression and negative outlook
- Anxiety and panic attacks
- Psychic numbing and disconnection
- Irritability and agitation
- Substance abuse, addictions, eating disorders
- Physical problems, real or imagined

Difficulties with Trust and Intimacy

*"My friends tell me I have an intimacy
problem. But they don't really know me."*
— Gary Shandling

You will naturally fear what you do not know. I often think of how mourning requires a safe holding environment, a reliable sanctuary that is able to affirm all that we are and feel. If you experience loss and there has not been safety and encouragement to mourn, your trust in people and the world around you is naturally compromised. The result is that you fear intimacy and avoid closeness to others.

Many grief-carriers have taught me that they feel they are unlovable. Often, this becomes a self-fulfilling prophecy. This person may have an awareness of the need for love but at the same time feel unworthy of it. The reality is that this person feels unloved and this translates into "I am unlovable." The tragic result is often isolation and loneliness. Some of these people do get married or attempt to have close relationships, but still keep distance in an effort to stay safe.

Grief-carriers often feel, consciously or subconsciously, that others will leave them. If you have been abandoned in your need to mourn by significant people in your life, you naturally feel others will also abandon you. If you have tried to trust in the past and people betrayed the trust, you come to believe no one is trustworthy. You don't open your heart easily, and when you do, you fear others will misuse you and ultimately go away. So, it becomes safer to stay distant and closed off.

Depression and Negative Outlook

"Depression is nourished by a lifetime of ungrieved and unforgiven hurts."
— Penelope Sweet

Grief-carriers may experience a loss of the divine spark—that which gives purpose and meaning to our living. When the spirit is muted, there is an ongoing hampering of the capacity to live life with meaning and purpose. The result is often depression and a negative, cynical view of life.

Depression symptoms include sadness, inactivity, difficulty with thinking and concentrating, a significant increase or decrease in appetite, sleep disturbance, feelings of hopelessness and dejection, and sometimes suicidal thoughts or actions. While there are multiple causes of depression, experience suggests that carried grief is a contributor for many people.

Depression sometimes masks itself in a general negative outlook on life. While some grief-carriers don't experience deep, dark depression, they suffer from a chronic, low-grade depression; the world begins to look gray. They lose their full range of emotional functioning, defending against ever being really happy or really sad. Sometimes they rationalize this mood state, as "this is just what life is like."

Similarly, feelings of meaninglessness often pervade the lives of grief-carriers. People who grieve but don't mourn often feel isolated emotionally and lack a sense of meaning and purpose. They experience a sense of soullessness, or a loss of vitality and enthusiasm for life and living. They feel empty and alone.

Anxiety and Panic Attacks

"Anxiety is fear of one's self."
— Wilhelm Stekel

Some grief-carriers struggle with a persistent and generalized anxiety. Anxiety is often reflected in motor tension (fatigue, muscle aches, easy startle response); autonomic hyperactivity (dry mouth, gastrointestinal distress, heart racing); apprehensive expectations (fears of injury or death); and hyper-vigilance and scanning (hyper-alertness, irritability, and problems with sleep disturbance). Again, just as with depression, there can be multiple causes of anxiety; however, I am certain that carried pain is a contributor for many people.

Anxiety sometimes shows up in the form of panic attacks. Panic is a sudden, overpowering fright. On occasion, these attacks may last for hours, though attacks are typically for a period of minutes, during which the person literally experiences terror. Panic attacks are often recurrent and episodic, though for some people they become chronic.

The human spirit must be connected to others and surrounded in unconditional love. I have seen numerous people in counseling whose panic attacks were the doorway to get them to give attention to carried grief and learn to authentically mourn.

Psychic Numbing and Disconnection

"Disconnecting from change does not recapture the past. It loses the future."
— Kathleen Norris

While shock and numbness are normal responses in the face of loss, some grief-carriers get so detached that they literally feel disconnected from the world around them. If this is happening to you, you may notice that you can see and hear others around you, but you can't feel them.

The result is that the world and the people in it seem unreal. You may live your days feeling you are in a daze, going through the motions yet not feeling present to others and even yourself. Some people describe this as a dream-like state with feelings of unreality. You are existing but not really alive to what is going on around you.

When you live in a state of numbness, you are not fully engaged. Although you may be physically doing some activity, your mind is elsewhere. Short-term memory loss and confusion often are a part of this experience.

Essentially, you are zoned out and "nobody's home." Grief-carriers have taught me that numbing is an attempt not to feel any pain (or any intense feelings for that matter). Of course, the result is being out of touch with one's deeper self, begging the question, "Is this what life is like?"

Numbing results in a feeling of existing but not really living. The muting power of numbness prevents you from experiencing any of the positive things that may be going on around you. You are literally disconnected from the world and yourself.

Irritability and Agitation

*"Minds that are ill at ease are agitated
by both hope and fear."*
— Ovid

Some grief-carriers express their pain indirectly through irritability and agitation. These symptoms may show up at work, at home, or anywhere they can find expression. It is like you are in a pressure cooker, and you are trying to release the pressure. In its extreme form, this symptom may show up as uncontrolled anger or rage.

These emotions of protest are often an unconscious attempt to fight off the underlying, more primary emotions of pain, helplessness, hurt, isolation and aloneness. People around you who sense or experience your irritability and agitation avoid you, resulting in more carried pain and less authentic mourning.

Substance Abuse, Addictions, Eating Disorders

*"You do anything long enough to escape the habit
of living until the escape becomes the habit."*
— David Ryan

Many grief-carriers will self-treat their pain
through substance abuse, addictive behaviors
and eating disorders. Modern society provides an
increasing number of substances that might be
abused. People are usually abusive of or addicted
to a specific substance such as alcohol, cocaine, or
food. However, grief-carriers can also be addicted
to activities, such as destructive relationships, sex,
smoking, gambling, work, exercise, achievement,
over-caretaking of others, religiosity, and
materialism. These substances and activities are
ways the person tries to move away from or deny
the pain of life losses.

Addictions serve to numb the grief-carrier's
feelings, sapping your spirit or "life force," and
locking you into living a life that feels muted and
lacking in purpose and positive direction. Self-
treating carried pain through addictions prevents

you from deeper satisfactions and any kind of spiritual fulfillment.

Addictions become the defense against the pain and necessary integration of life losses. The capacity to try to make oneself feel good through chemicals or activities creates a false sense of mastery or control. Lacking control of the pain of grief, the addictions are often unconscious attempts to take control over something. Unfortunately, many addictions result in a slow but steady process of self-destruction.

Physical Problems, Real or Imagined

"Your lifestyle—how you live, eat, emote, and
think—determines your health. To prevent
disease, you may have to change how you live."
— Brian Carter

If we don't mourn one way, it comes out another. Many grief-carriers store the pain in their bodies. The result is that the immune system breaks down and illness surfaces. Many formal studies have documented significant increases in illness following the experience of a variety of losses in life, particularly death loss.

When we authentically mourn, these physical symptoms are normal and temporary. However, when people shut down, deny or inhibit mourning, they sometimes assume a "sick role" in an effort to legitimize not feeling well to those around them. They "somaticize" their feelings of grief, which means they unconsciously turn their emotional and spiritual hurts into physical ones. This often results in frequent visits to the physician's office. Sometimes the physical symptoms are very real; other times they are imagined. These imagined symptoms are often a silent voice crying out for the need to give expression to the carried pain. The imagined illnesses usually express themselves through multiple symptoms and complaints, usually presented in a vague fashion. Typically, there are no organic findings to support a physical diagnosis.

The somaticizer may become so completely preoccupied with bodily involvement and sickness that she has little or no energy to relate to others and to do the work of mourning. Even in the absence of real illness and emotional support from medical caregivers, no amount of reassurance or logic convinces her she is not. The unconscious need to protect oneself requires that this person desperately needs the belief in illness to mask feelings connected to the loss and grief.

We should note that this somaticizing is different than the person who experiences real physical illness during the mourning process. Some degree of physical disturbance is a common dimension of the normal grief process. As caregivers we would never want to automatically assume that a grieving person is converting all of his emotions into physical symptoms. Numerous investigations have documented a definite tendency for grievers to be more sick than the general population. A general medical examination for anyone who has experienced a life loss is always an excellent standard of care.

However, somaticizing grief as the chief mechanism of mourning is a means of avoiding grief. You may truly feel sick, but medically speaking there is not anything really wrong with you physically. Quite simply, life cannot reinhabit the body until we mourn our life losses. The result is that you can feel sick, if not dead, while you are alive. The good news is that carried griefs stored in the body can be integrated into life as long as their causes are not denied. When you soften to the pain, the body relaxes and converts suffering into healing.

Grief Avoidance Response Styles

"The only way to the other side is through."
— Helen Keller

Now let's look at a number of grief avoidance response styles. These are dominant behavior patterns that tend to seem to define the person they are affecting. Of course, this list doesn't describe every possible grief avoidance response style, just some of the most common.

Common grief avoidance response styles
The Displacer
The Replacer
The Postponer
The Minimizer/Intellectualizer
The Chemical Abuser
The Worker
The Shopper
The Traveler
The Eater
The Crusader
The Perpetual Griever

The Displacer

"Anger is a signal, and one worth listening to."
— Harriet Lerner

The displacer is the person who takes the expression of his grief away from the loss itself and places the feelings in other directions. For example, while not acknowledging the feelings of grief, the person may complain of difficulty at work or in relationships with other people. Another example is the person who appears to be chronically agitated and upset at even the most minor of events. While some awareness may be present, displacing usually occurs totally unconsciously.

Some persons who adopt the displacer orientation become bitter toward life in general. Others displace the bitter unconscious expression of their grief inward, becoming full of self-hatred and experiencing debilitating depression. So, while at times these people displace their grief in interactions with other people, at other times they believe that other people dislike them, once again projecting unhappiness from the inside to the outside.

The main intent of the displacer is to shift away feelings from their source and onto a less threatening person, place or situation. Personal relationships often become stressed and strained for the displacer, who is unable to acknowledge the occurrence of this common pattern of grief avoidance.

The Replacer

"I fooled myself into thinking that if I
remarried I would stop missing her.
Obviously I remarried too quickly, but
nobody could tell me that at the time."
— Anonymous

The replacer is the person who takes the emotions
that were invested in a relationship that ended
in death and reinvests them prematurely in
another relationship. Again, there is little, if any,
conscious awareness for replacers about how their
efforts are really a means of avoiding the work
of grief.

Observers will sometimes assume the replacer must
not have loved the person who died all that much
if he can so quickly become involved in a new
relationship. In actuality, the replacer has often
loved very much, and out of a need to overcome
the pain of confronting feelings related to the loss,
moves into an avoidance pattern of replacement.

The Postponer

> *"We forget that every good that is worth*
> *possessing must be paid for in strokes of*
> *daily effort. We postpone and postpone,*
> *until those smiling possibilities are dead."*
> — William James

The postponer is the person who believes that if you delay the expression of your grief, over time it will hopefully go away. Obviously, it does not. The grief builds up within and typically comes out in a variety of ways that do not best serve your needs.

The postponer may feel that if the grief doesn't vanish, at least there may come a point in time when it will feel safer to experience the pain. Unaware that through expression comes healing, she continues to postpone. The grief builds up inside her, pushing toward the point of explosion, making her feel even less capable of experiencing feelings related to loss.

Without self-awareness or intervention, a vicious cycle is firmly rooted in place. Often the more the person senses grief yearning for expression, the more an effort is made to postpone or put it off.

Postponing is frequently an automatic unconscious process. A few people will consciously acknowledge this pattern with comments like, "I just don't want to grieve right now. I'll think about it later." However, the majority of people do not know they are postponing the work of their grief. They initiate this pattern of avoidance quietly and quickly, and society often rewards them for "doing very well" with their grief.

The Minimizer/Intellectualizer

> "To tackle a problem intellectually is very
> easy. But to tackle a problem existentially...
> not just to think about it, but to live it
> through, to go through it, to allow yourself
> to be transformed through it...is difficult."
> — Osho

The minimizer/intellectualizer is the person who is aware of feelings of grief, but, when they are felt, works to minimize the feelings by diluting them through a variety of rationalizations. This person attempts to prove to himself that he is not really impacted by the loss. Observers of minimizers may hear them talk about how well they are doing and how they are back to their normal routine.

On a conscious level, this person's minimizations may seem to be working and certainly conform to society's urgings to quickly "get over" grief. However, internally the repressed feelings of grief build and emotional strain results.

This person often believes that grief is something to be quickly thought through but not felt through. This is typically an intellectual process in which words become a substitute for the expression of authentic feelings. Any feelings of grief are very threatening to the minimizer, who seeks to avoid pain at all cost.

Unfortunately, the more this person works to convince herself that the feelings of grief have been "overcome," the more crippled she becomes in allowing for emotional expression. The result is the evolution of a destructive, vicious cycle.

The Chemical Abuser

> *"When I drank I could stop feeling my sadness*
> *for a while. But eventually, it took me over*
> *and destroyed me and everyone in my family."*
> — Anonymous

The chemical abuser is the person who uses alcohol and/or other drugs to avoid the work of mourning. Interestingly, this behavior is often reinforced with comments like, "Here, take this, it will make you feel better." It is no accident that chemical abuse is a common problem for many grieving people.

Experience suggests that chemical abuse is among the most dangerous of avoidance patterns. Many people experiencing grief are greeted with "sage" advice that alcohol, in particular, will improve their mood, block out painful memories, and help them sleep better. Yet patterns of abuse may lead to significant drinking problems.

The reality is that patterns of alcohol abuse cause disruptive sleep patterns, worsening mood states, and increasing agitation. Chemical abuse can become a destructive pattern of behavior that blocks the work of mourning for years into the future.

The Worker

"Work addiction, although it is the most accepted and encouraged of all addictions, is a serious disease that destroys relationships and kills people."
— Bryan E. Robinson

The worker is the person who begins to over-invest in work to the point where no time is available to think about or feel the loss. Interestingly enough, the worker is often following the advice of well-wishers who encourage him to "keep busy." Making matters worse, many people are already work-addicted prior to a loss.

Prior work-addiction creates the same approach to grief work—to hurry up and rush through it. Such an approach is self-defeating because healing in grief cannot be rushed and should not be avoided. Paradoxically, grieving people who throw themselves into work ultimately hurt more when they compulsively try to hurt less.

An example of this is a man I recently saw in my practice who, following the death of his wife, found himself working 18 to 20 hours a day. It became apparent that he was funneling all of the emotions related to his wife's death into and through his work. Once the pattern was acknowledged for the need it was serving in him, he could begin to do the work of his mourning in healthy, life-giving ways.

The Shopper

> *"I couldn't stop myself from shopping. It was only later that I realized I was trying to spend away my pain and feelings of loss."*
> — Anonymous

The shopper is the person who spends money in efforts to avoid the work of mourning. I often refer to this pattern as "retail therapy." This indulgence usually only provides short-term relief before another fix is needed.

Some grieving people get themselves into serious financial problems when they spend beyond their resources. Some people rationalize the behavior as "being good to myself" as they spiral into massive problems with debt. Secondary grief arrives in the mail within 30 days of the shopping binge—the bill arrives!

The Traveler

"Sometimes I figured if I just kept moving, I'd never land. And if I never landed, I'd never feel."
— Anonymous

The traveler is the person who stays on the move to avoid the work of mourning. Again, this person's behavior is reinforced with comments like, "What you need to do is get away, take a trip." The message is that you can leave your grief behind, and so that is what this person tries to achieve.

Some grieving people don't just travel but prematurely move their place of residence. This usually creates secondary losses of previous support systems and comforting routines. Paradoxically, the traveler or mover may begin to miss what was left behind, the very things that she was trying to escape.

The Eater

> *"Instead of acknowledging my feelings of loss
> and emptiness after my divorce, I just ate
> everything I could get my hands on."*
> — Anne Johnson

The eater is the person who has continual cravings for food. We know that stress denied often stimulates hunger centers in the brain. Experience suggests that the craving is often experienced as a compulsion, and the person feels powerless to stop eating. Unconsciously the eater may be trying to fill a void from the emptiness felt inside his body.

The eater may observe that he is continuing to gain weight, yet he is not able to change the behavior. As they avoid the work of mourning, eaters compound their problems with physical and emotional problems secondary to weight gain.

Some grief-carriers have also taught me that another consequence of inhibited mourning may be anorexia nervosa or bulimia. Again, I would caution that while there can be many causes of eating disorders, experience suggests that carried pain is sometimes a contributor.

In-depth exploration of eating disorders is way beyond the scope of this book. For our purposes, I would note that the essential features of anorexia nervosa are intense concerns with being overweight and a persistent feeling of being fat, even when weight loss has begun or has even been substantial. This is combined with a refusal to maintain body weight at the minimally appropriate level, considering age and height, and evidence of a weight loss of at least 25 percent from the original weight.

The converse pattern from anorexia nervosa is bulimia, a chronic pattern of binge eating. Bulimia is known as the gorge-purge syndrome. The main features are recurrent binge eating combined with depression and remorse following the binges, with awareness that the pattern of this behavior is not right but cannot be stopped.

The Crusader

> *"I was helping everyone all the time. I got so
> busy helping them I forgot to help myself.
> It was like I was running from me!"*
> — Linda Billings

The crusader is the person who converts her grief into over-dedication or premature involvement with a cause. Again, this behavior is often reinforced with comments like, "Helping others will help you." Of course the person who encourages this kind of action prematurely is distracting the mourner from the work she needs to do.

The causes the crusader might get involved with are easy to get passionate about: stricter laws for drunk drivers, establishment of support groups for bereaved people, etc. The problem is that premature over-involvement in a cause, regardless of how important the cause may be, can inhibit and delay one's own work of mourning.

The Perpetual Griever

*"If my grief softens I'm afraid I'll have
to admit he is never coming back. And
that is what I don't want to face."*
— A workshop participant

While the Postponer puts off embracing his grief,
the Perpetual Griever embraces his grief too tightly
for too long. He begins to move through the Needs
of Mourning (see p. 115), acknowledging the reality
of the death and embracing the pain of the loss,
but he seems to get stuck there. Many Perpetual
Grievers get stuck out of feelings of loyalty to the
person who died. "If I start to feel better," they
think, consciously or subconsciously, "then I'm
being disloyal to the person who died. If I start to
feel better, it means I'm not loving the person as
much as I should." As a result, Perpetual Grievers
suffer from chronic, long-term sorrow.

We should note here that perpetual grief arises not
only from death loss. Perpetual grief may also stem
from loss from abuse or other trauma. Survivors
of sexual abuse, for example, may carry their pain
perpetually out of feelings of guilt. On some level
they may feel they deserve to suffer because of

d complicity in the abuse. Of course,
ver their fault, but it is common for
artly is.

While grief never ends and you will always feel
some pain over your losses, your grief should
soften as you mourn it. Over time, feelings of
happiness should begin to outweigh feelings of
deep sadness.

So these are some of the more common symptoms I
have observed in people who carry the pain of grief
and have not had the opportunity, permission or
companionship to authentically mourn. I do not
describe these symptoms to shame you or anyone
else. I describe them to open you to the possibility
of how carried pain might be impacting your life.

Fortunately, underneath grief avoidance resides a
sense for many people that life could be different.
This sense may exist at a subconscious level,
but with insight, support and encouragement,
conscious mourning can and will take place. It's
at this point that you can begin transitioning away
from avoidance and into the wilderness of grief

in ways that ultimately result in healing and a life filled with meaning and purpose.

Once recognized for what they are, these symptoms can be listened to in a whole new way. When we allow ourselves to stay open to our mourning instead of closing around it, we can begin to experience an integration of it that breaks our pattern of retreating from pain and from life itself. Authentic mourning connects us to our deepest selves, others and the world around us.

Carried Grief Self-Inventory

> *"One heals suffering only by*
> *experiencing it to the full."*
> — Marcel Proust

Now that you've explored some of the common symptoms of carried grief—and perhaps recognized yourself here and there, I'd like you to consider the possible sources of your carried pain. As you work to make a commitment to have the courage to proclaim your right to heal, get the help you need, and integrate the pain into your life, you may find it helpful to review the following Carried Grief Self-Inventory.

Again, the purpose of inventorying your losses and acknowledging these potential symptoms is not to discourage or shame you, but to ultimately empower you. This self-inventory is a way for you to begin to recognize and acknowledge your experience. Yes, this process can be frightening. After all, while committing yourself to healing ultimately brings a better life, it also threatens to forever alter life as you have known it. You may find that one part of you wants to heal while another resists change. Obviously, my hope is that you will have the courage to "do your work" and discover a new, more meaning-filled life.

The following Loss Inventory lists many types of losses commonly suffered by humankind. I invite you to skim the list and circle or put a check-mark next to the types of losses that you have experienced. This list is not comprehensive, of course, so I'd also like you to use the blank lines at the end to write down all the significant losses in your life, including those that may not be listed here.

Loss of People You Love

Separation (physical and/or emotional)
Rejection
Hostility/Grudges
Illness (such as Alzheimer's, debilitating conditions)
Divorce
Abandonment/betrayal
Death
Empty nest

Loss of Pets

Loss of Aspects of Self

Self-esteem (often through physical, sexual or
    emotional abuse or rape, humiliation, rejection or
    neglect)
Health, physical or mental ability
Job (downsizing, firing, failed business, retirement)
Control (such as through addiction, victimization)
Innocence (such as through abuse, exposure to
    immoral behavior)
Sexual identity/ability/desire
Security (such as through financial problems, war)
Expectations about how our lives should/would be
Reputation
Beliefs (religious, spiritual, belief in others we trusted)
Dreams (cherished hopes for the future)

Loss of Physical Objects

Home (such as through a physical disaster, move or transition into assisted living environments)

Linking objects (special items such as photos that carry emotional weight)

Money

Belongings (through theft or fire, etc.)

Nature/place (through a move, changing land use)

Loss through Developmental Transitions

Toddlerhood to childhood

Childhood to adolescence

Adolescence to adulthood

Leaving home

Marriage

Having/not having children

Mid-life

Taking care of parents

Retirement

Old age

My personal loss inventory:

_____

_____

_____

_____

_____

_____

_____

_____

_____

_____

_____

_____

_____

_____

_____

_____

_____

After you've completed your personal loss inventory, go back and circle or highlight those losses that you think may be contributing to your carried pain. How do you know which are most significant for you? As you're perusing your list, pause for a moment on each item and note which elicit the most emotion. Which make you feel the most sad? The most angry? The most fear? The most pain? Whether they seem significant on the surface or not, these are likely your deepest sources of carried grief. For example, having been fired from a job may, for you, have resulted in more carried pain than the death of a family member, especially if you mourned the death but never the job loss.

Now that you've inventoried the types of losses you've experienced in your life, I encourage you to answer the following questions.

Circle the word that most applies to how you authentically feel.

1. Do you have difficulties with trust and intimacy?

   Never Seldom Occasionally Often Usually

2. Do you have a tendency toward depression and a negative outlook?

   Never Seldom Occasionally Often Usually

3. Do you have difficulties with anxiety and/or panic attacks?

   Never Seldom Occasionally Often Usually

4. Do you have trouble with psychic numbing and disconnection?

   Never Seldom Occasionally Often Usually

5. Do you have difficulties with irritability and agitation?

   Never Seldom Occasionally Often Usually

6. Do you struggle with substance abuse, addictions or eating disorders?

   Never Seldom Occasionally Often Usually

7. Do you have any physical problems, real or imagined?

   Never Seldom Occasionally Often Usually

8. Do you see yourself living out aspects of the grief avoidance response styles outlined in this section?

   Never Seldom Occasionally Often Usually

9. Do you find it easier to take care of others than you do to care for yourself?

   Never Seldom Occasionally Often Usually

10. Do you find it difficult to express your feelings?

    Never Seldom Occasionally Often Usually

11. Do you find it difficult to ask for what you want from other people?

    Never Seldom Occasionally Often Usually

12. Do you feel a lack of meaning and purpose in your life?

    Never Seldom Occasionally Often Usually

If you answered "Occasionally," "Often" or "Usually" to any of these questions, you are probably living in the shadow of the ghosts of grief. Acknowledging and authentically mourning your grief will take time, commitment and discipline. But, the good news is that you must want to do it or you wouldn't be reading this book. Your life exactly as it is contains just what is needed for your own journey of healing the carried pain of grief. Go forth with courage!

Part Four

How to heal your carried grief

"Change is a door that can only
be opened from the inside."
— Terry Mitchell

Becoming aware that you are living in the shadow
of the ghosts of grief and then working to banish
the ghosts is at the heart of your healing. The
healing process is a continuum. It begins with
an awareness that you have carried pain, and it
evolves to experiencing a meaning-filled life. And
in between is the focus of this section of this book:
the healing process.

Healing carried pain is not a random experience.
Healing requires that you identify and befriend
your carried pain. You must openly acknowledge
the presence of something important that deserves
your attention.

Without doubt, we have all heard, perhaps even
said, the tired cliché "time heals all wounds."
Yet, time alone has nothing to do with healing.
To heal, we must be willing to enter into our
griefs—to befriend them. And even then, our

life losses are never "fixed" or "resolved;" they can only be soothed and integrated through actively experiencing the mixture of thoughts and feelings involved.

Grief is like a spiral. Spirals are unending and amorphous. You can go through the same circuit again and again, but traveling up the spiral you pass through them at a different level, experiencing a slightly different perspective each time. They do not form discrete, static shapes because spirals can always grow and change.

The gradual movement toward transformation invites emotional, spiritual and interpersonal growth. With the support of a "compassionate companion" (see p. 107), your capacity to reveal your losses and make deep and lasting changes becomes possible.

I have had the honor of working with hundreds of people who have allowed me to support them in mourning life losses that originate from carried pain. I use the term "catch-up mourning" to

Catch-up Mourning: Going backward and giving attention to any grief you have carried from past losses in your life. The purpose of going back and doing your grief work is anchored in eventually freeing you to go forward with newfound meaning and purpose in your life, living and loving.

describe the process that helps them experience a more considered, conscious life, rather than just drifting in a fog or living out their carried pain.

A model I have created to help in this process is outlined below. The entire premise of helping my fellow human beings do catch-up mourning is my belief that when we learn to be with the pain that we have denied, we retrieve those parts of ourselves that were left behind. The result is that we are able to accept and integrate those parts of ourselves. We discover that in giving voice to our mourning lies the wisdom we need to live a meaningful, purposeful life. If you mourn your carried pain, you can truly live until you die.

In the broadest sense, deciding to address your carried pain is a choice between opposites: a life devoid of deep feeling or a deeply felt life; escapist activities or meaningful activities. It means choosing between experiencing a life with its very real pains and pleasures or living in an anesthetized fog where authentic feelings are inhibited; between a consciousness of our deepest feelings, or a vague, muted self-awareness. Giving attention to your carried pain is, in many ways, choosing between living life from a place of truth or living a lie. When you are living a lie, you are misrepresenting the reality of your experience or the truth of your being. You are allowing a disconnect between the self within and the self manifested in the world around you.

For example, you are living a lie when you say you are angry but the truth is you are afraid. When you laugh when you need to cry. When you present yourself as having values you do not feel or hold. When you pretend a love you do not feel. When you are kind to everyone except the persons you claim to love. When you claim beliefs to win acceptance.

When you end up living a lie, you are always your own first victim because the fraud is ultimately directed at yourself. If you are living a series of lies, you do so because you feel or believe that who you really are is not acceptable. You value a delusion in someone else's mind above your own knowledge of the truth. The result is living an incongruent life and experiencing the carried grief symptoms outlined in Part Three of this book.

As I've said, our mourning-avoidant culture invites you to carry pain and encourages you to live an unauthentic life. You may have been influenced in ways that up until now have made an appreciation of authentically mourning life losses all but impossible. So if you are living in the shadow of the ghosts of grief, stop shaming yourself! You may have learned early in life to deny feelings of loss and to wear a mask, and eventually you lost contact with your inner self. You may have become unconscious to much of your inner self in adjusting to the world around you.

Significant adults in your childhood may have encouraged you to disown fear, grief, anger and pain because such feelings made them uncomfortable. Adults who carry grief tend to create children who carry grief, not only through direct communication, but through their own behavior, which proclaims to the child what is appropriate, proper, and acceptable.

The paradox is that in order to live in this environment, you may have learned to "play dead" as a way of making life more tolerable. Playing dead is so common for many grief-carriers that it becomes your perception of normal. It is the familiar, the comfortable, whereas living "alive" can feel strange, even disorienting. Sadly, playing dead is a policy of self-rejection and self-estrangement, and if you are living in the shadow of the ghosts of grief, you have joined the ranks of what I call the "living dead."

By honoring the presence of our current and carried grief, by coming to surrender to the appropriateness of experiencing our grief losses, we are, in fact, committing ourselves to facing the pain. We are committing ourselves to paying attention to our anguish in ways that allow us to begin to breathe life into our soul again.

In this book, I hope you find encouragement to gently and with self-compassion befriend your grief. Yes, as strange as it may seem, you must make it your friend. Instead of pulling down the blinds and shutting out light and love, I will invite you to come out of the darkness and into the light. Slowly, and in the presence of compassionate companions, you can and will return to life (or experience it deeply for the first time!) and begin living and loving in ways that put stars into your sky!

Deciding to Go on a Journey:
A Model for "Catch-up" Mourning

"The pain passes, but the beauty remains."
— Pierre Auguste Renoir

So how do you heal your carried grief? How do you do catch-up mourning? The rest of this chapter is dedicated to helping you figure out how to authentically mourn your carried grief so that you can go on to live and love fully.

Healing your carried grief: a four-step model
Step 1: Acknowledging your carried grief
Step 2: Overcoming resistance to do the work
Step 3: Actively mourning your carried grief
Step 4: Integrating your carried grief

Step 1: Acknowledging Your Carried Grief

"There is not grief that does not speak."
— Henry Wordsworth Longfellow

At the end of Part Three, I asked you to inventory the potential sources of your carried grief and to begin to recognize in yourself the symptoms of carried grief. If you completed the Carried Grief Self-Inventory, you have begun the first step to healing. Self-awareness and acknowledgement is the first step in deciding to face your carried grief and to change your life. Even though your life path has been shaped by carried grief, you are deciding you no longer need to be defined by it. You are choosing to be an active participant in your healing.

Yet, the decision to heal is not as simple as it may sound. Actually, it is a decision you have to make again and again. Each step in the healing process presents new challenges, fears, and opportunities. Every time you give attention to that which needs your attention, you reinforce your commitment to the healing process.

Step 2: Overcoming Resistance to Do the Work

"To venture causes anxiety. Not to venture is to lose oneself."
— Soren Kierkegaard

Approaching feelings that have been inhibited or denied can be a naturally difficult experience.

When you first begin to feel some intense emotions surrounding carried grief, you might well fear that your pain will be limitless. Many people I have helped over the years have told me some variation on, "If I let myself start to feel, I may never stop." However, opening the door to carried pain, while often frightening, is necessary in the healing process.

Obviously, to begin to admit to having such frightening and powerful emotions undermines any denial that one is "just fine." And remember, many people around you, and society in general, would like it if you were "just fine." Sometimes when you start to do catch-up mourning, some people in your life will label you as having problems or being emotionally unstable.

In fact, what you are doing is openly acknowledging the presence of something important that deserves your attention. Each step in this process will require your courage to refuse to give into your fears. Still, you may be tempted to take the path of least resistance, to return to your defenses and ignore the feelings within that are inviting you to acknowledge and honor them.

Yes, honor them. Honoring literally means "recognizing the value of and respecting." To honor your emotional and spiritual life is not self-destructive or harmful, it is self-sustaining and life-giving.

You must set your intention to mourn your carried grief. Having intention is defined as being conscious of what you want to experience. When you set your intention to heal unhealed wounds, you make a true commitment to positively influence the work that must be done. Essentially, you choose between living an unlived life and becoming an active participant in your catch-up mourning.

Your decision to heal is a moment-by-moment, day-by-day choice. You take one small step forward, you commit to one particular action, and then you take the next step. By saying yes in the moment, you gradually create momentum toward your healing: "Yes, I will go find a good counselor today."

If you can see yourself in the center of your own healing process, able to make choices that will serve you well in the long-term, it's easier to make the commitment to heal. Realizing that you are in control, that you will not be forced to do anything against your will, is critical to feeling safe as you do your work. Paradoxically, when you are assured that your "No, I'm not ready" will be respected, you experience the unfolding of being able to one day say, "Yes, I am ready."

Being in control of dosing your pain is the opposite of what happened when your grief was denied you. Now you can make choices. Reliving painful feelings and taking risks are part of the healing process. But your desire to make choices lets you ask yourself, "Is this the right time? Am I willing to go through this now? Do I want to open up to my carried pain or do I want to shut down and continue to live in the shadow of the ghosts?"

The decision to do your work related to carried pain is personal and unique. Later in this section, I am going to ask you to express your decision to do this work. Keeping that in mind, look at how one person expressed the decision to mourn her carried grief:

I have decided to give attention to my pain, to feel the feelings I have tried to keep away. I don't want to continue living the way I have been. I am going to choose the truth and free myself to discover peace in my heart. I have the strength and desire to do my work and free myself to live with new meaning and purpose in life.

The nice thing about creating a written statement such as this one is that this person could then refer back to this statement as she did her work of mourning. When she needed motivation, she would re-read her commitment and continue with her journey toward healing.

By honoring the presence of your carried pain, you are committing yourself to facing the pain. You are committing yourself to paying attention to that which needs to be given attention in ways that will ultimately allow you to breathe life into your spirit. Yes, with the support of a compassionate companion, you have the opportunity to experience the unfolding of your healing. So recognize your natural resistance, but go forward with courage and commitment.

Making Your Decision

If you are ready to commit yourself to the decision to do the work of mourning your carried grief, use the space below to write out your very own statement. Keep it available to remind yourself of the importance of this new direction you are taking in your life.

_____

_____

_____

_____

_____

_____

Step 3: Actively Mourning Your Carried Grief

*"A wound that goes unacknowledged and
unwept is a wound that cannot heal."*
— John Eldredge

Actively mourning your carried grief is the most painful step toward stepping out of the shadow of the ghosts of grief and into the light, but also the most liberating. Remember that the word *grief* means the constellation of internal thoughts and feelings you experience within yourself about a loss, while *mourning* is when you take the grief you have on the inside and express it outside of yourself. Mourning is "grief gone public" or "the outward expression of grief."

On the one hand, the recognition that you have carried pain from life losses naturally brings sorrow. On the other hand, the discovery that it is never too late to mourn creates the energy to actually do the work necessary to heal and create a meaning-filled life.

Our feelings are the way we perceive ourselves. They are our response to the world around us and how we know we are alive. That is why when you shut them down you risk being among the living dead. When you lose touch with your feelings, you have no true awareness of life. Feelings are a vital link in your relationship to others, yourself and the world around you. Obviously, a way out of your carried grief is to identify and experience your feelings in ways that integrate them into your life.

When you are mourning, you need permission, validation and the space to feel. You need sanctuary, which is a place of refuge from external demands. A space where you are free to disengage from the outside world. A place where your need to turn inward and suspend will not be hurried or ridiculed. Obviously, finding sanctuary in an environment that often discourages the open expression of grief can be difficult, at times almost impossible.

That is why I ask you to find what I describe as a "compassionate companion" to help you as you do your work.

Finding a Compassionate Companion

I do not pretend that to openly mourn our life losses is done easily and efficiently. It is not easy to befriend the griefs that knock on our hearts. Many of us have carried our pain for years. So, healing from carried grief is something no one should try to do alone. Indeed, in most situations doing so is almost impossible, and virtually every grief-carrier can benefit from the right kind of help. Notice I said "the right kind." Before setting off to put to work the principles explored in this section, I encourage you read the section entitled "Choosing a counselor" (p. 112).

I believe deep in my soul that a blessing we seek in mourning our life losses is not to live in the absence of pain. It is to live "alive" in a way that our pain has meaning. To search for and discover this meaning in our current buck-up culture, we need compassionate companions—grief caregivers who do not perceive the emotions of grief as inappropriate but see them as a necessary and normal response to life losses. In this context, compassionate companions are trained counselors (ideally with specialized training and/ or background in grief and loss counseling) who recognize that supporting you in your need to mourn is not about assessing, analyzing, fixing or resolving your grief. Instead, they know it is about being totally present to you, even being a temporary guardian of your soul.

Compassionate companions are willing and able to help you with your carried pain and give attention to that which you need to give attention to. They are very sensitive to the consequences that carried pain can have. They possess a natural empathy and unconditional love as they help you gain an understanding of how your symptoms of carried pain are a result of your history rather than some unknown source.

In fact, the word compassion implies an active sharing of experience. Compassion is made up of two parts: *com* for "with" and *passion*, which connotes energy, emotion or intense activity. As you give expression to your carried pain with a compassionate companion, you create positive energy and actively participate in the work of mourning.

For me, compassionate companions are those caregivers who have explored their own history of life losses and had the courage to experience their own authentic mourning in ways that allow them to achieve their integrity rather than projecting the need to exercise power over their clients. Only when compassionate companions have done their own mourning work will they be able to provide you with the perspective you need to experience and express your own loss history. In addition, they recognize they have an obligation, once they help you access your need to convert passive grief to active mourning, to stay present to you as your experience unfolds. In other words, they serve as a bridge to getting you the resources you need to do your work of mourning.

The helping model of a compassionate companion is anchored in a "teach me" perspective. They are aware they are learning from and observing you, not treating you. Observance means not only "to watch out for" but also "to keep and honor" and "to bear witness." The caregiver you will feel safe with realizes that for you to feel safe, you must feel you are in the presence of someone working with a cleaned-out, caring heart. It is this open heart that allows the caregiver to be completely present to you.

A central role of the compassionate companion is the art of honoring your life stories surrounding loss. To honor your story requires that your caregiver go slowly and really listen as you acknowledge the reality of your losses, review memories and discover meaning in your continued living. Your caregiver realizes that you must go backward and give attention to your losses before you can go forward.

I recognize that finding compassionate companions in contemporary times is not always easy. Many people (including trained mental health caregivers) may not know how to truly listen, really hear, and realize how to honor your stories of loss. Sometimes finding a compassionate companion

Group Therapy for Carried Grief

Experience suggests that an excellent tool
for healing carried grief is the small therapy
group of five to ten people. The process
often becomes less of a group process than
individual counseling done in a group context.
Preferably, the group should have two
therapist-facilitators, which enables them to
plan meetings and de-brief together.

Using the group's insight often becomes
invaluable as members work on their core
issues related to carried grief. Each person
can share his or her unique journey in a non-
threatening "safe place." Commonly, group
members benefit from seeing an individual
therapist as well as participating in the group
experience.

Special note to therapists: We offer trainings
at the Center for Loss and Life Transition
that can assist you in establishing groups
to assist people in healing carried grief.
See www.centerforloss.com for details.

takes more than a little work, but I assure you it is worth the search. A recommendation from someone you trust is probably the best place to start. Ultimately, though, only you will be able to determine if a particular caregiver can help you.

Choosing a Counselor

Finding a counselor or therapist who can help you with your carried grief takes some work, and then deciding if it is a good match takes even more.

In selecting a therapist, you have the right to shop around and ask questions. To do this you may need to overcome some of the passivity that sometimes is part and parcel of carried pain. However, it is critical to convince yourself that you deserve a therapist or group experience that is best matched to your needs.

• Training, Philosophy, Experience
  As you explore your options, feel free to ask about the counselor's education and training. What degrees has she earned?

What certifications or licenses does he hold? Reputable professionals will feel comfortable answering questions about their training, philosophy and experience. Do not hesitate to ask about their therapeutic philosophies and the kind of techniques they might use in counseling you. Describe your issues of carried grief and ask how they might work with you.

Unfortunately, there are some therapists who should be avoided. Even highly qualified professionals may simply not have worked with or had experience in the area of carried grief. That does not make them less competent; it may simply mean they are not a good match for you and your needs. Again, it is legitimate to ask a counselor about her experience with carried grief. Ask her how many similar clients she has seen.

- Relationship
  While this is a very subjective area, the question is: Does this person seem like someone you would be able to work with effectively? Does

her personality, answers to your questions and concerns, and office environment make you feel safe and respected? Do you sense that he genuinely cares about you as a human being and about the work you are going to be doing together? Essentially, do you feel comfortable with this person and sense that she can help you? If it does not feel right, then it is probably not right for you. For additional guidelines on finding a good counselor, you may find it helpful to read Touchstone 8 in the book *Understanding Your Grief*, available from the Center for Loss and Life Transition.

A very wise person once said, "It is possible to listen a person's soul into existence." In my experience, effective counseling can be the soul's bridge back from living in the shadow of the ghosts to living a life in the light. With this little bit of information and the desire to find the right match for yourself, counseling can be a vital ingredient of your own healing journey.

If in the end, after reading this book, you determine you would benefit from authentically mourning your life losses, you will need and deserve calmness of spirit from those who companion you. As your caregiver watches out for you, enough safety needs to be present in ways that allow you to bear your pain and suffering while at the same time realizing that which you have lost has transformed you. Also, you need someone with a calmness of spirit who has hope and belief that you can and will live your life awake and on purpose!

How You Will Work With Your Compassionate Companion: The Needs of Mourning

> "The proper function of man is to live, not to exist. I shall not waste my days in trying to prolong them. I shall use my time."
> — Jack London

You may have already noticed that throughout this book I use the phrase "the work of mourning" because it is indeed hard work! And remember—

reading about this process is not a substitute for doing the work!

In my work with people grieving the death of someone loved, I use the concept of the "Needs of Mourning" to help them identify the central needs they must meet if they are to heal. These needs are also central to your experience as a catch-up mourner, whether you are carrying pain primarily from the death(s) of people you have loved or from other types of losses.

Need 1: Acknowledge the reality of the loss(es)

Your compassionate companion will be able to support you as you identify and name your losses that have resulted in carried grief, which you may have already begun to do if you completed the Carried Grief Self-Inventory at the end of Part Three. Some people can easily name their griefs, while others may struggle to do so. If you reflect on this reality, it only makes sense. Identifying carried griefs can be very difficult, particularly ones that may have been denied or "stuffed" for years. But if you do the work to identify and acknowledge the losses that have resulted in your carried grief, you have met the first need of mourning.

Need 2: Embrace the pain of the loss(es)

As you work with a compassionate companion, you will first identify your losses and then be gently supported as you truly experience the feelings connected with them. The function of your work is to help you go through instead of around or trying to avoid your grief as you may have been doing for some time now.

Actually, the word *feeling* comes from the Indo-European root that means "touch." To feel is to activate your capacity to be touched and changed by experiences that you encounter along life's path. This is what makes for the movement and flow of your life. The term *perturbation* refers to the capacity to experience change and movement. The purpose of mourning is to allow feelings to move through you in ways that integrate them into your life.

To integrate griefs into your life requires that you are touched by what you experience. When you cannot feel a feeling, you are closed in your ability to use it, and instead of experiencing perturbation, you become stuck. As we reviewed in Part Three of this book, this can result in being out of touch with your feelings and leads you down a path to carrying your grief.

While talking about your carried grief may be helpful, you may discover that talk therapy may not be enough to activate the expression of carried grief. That is why your compassionate companion will be familiar with experiential tools to help you activate and facilitate your catch-up mourning. These experiential tools will help you access the unconscious processes that otherwise may remain hidden from your ordinary awareness.

Examples of these tools might range from honoring your story in a safe environment to journaling to support group work. These and many other tools (art therapy, nature therapy and more) might be made use of in the context of a comprehensive approach to helping you, ideally under the guidance of a caregiver who is familiar with the principles of integrating carried grief.

And while methods that focus on the expression of feelings as the end goal of the healing work are beneficial, I believe the preferred approach is to combine emotional release with cognitive insight. In my experience, the best verifying evidence that you are on the right path to healing is increasing recognition and clarity of your feelings, which is the result of both insight and connection to your emotions. But always keep in mind that authentic catch-up mourning demands not just thinking, but feeling. Authentic healing does not take place in the context of intellectual insight in isolation. In other words, you might experience a wealth of insight without integrating your deeper feelings. True healing of carried pain is ultimately an emotional and spiritual journey with insight only serving as a road map.

Each time you experience and release some of your carried pain, you will gain confidence in your capacity to regroup after a period of emotional and spiritual work with your compassionate companion. Slowly, and with no rewards for speed, you can come to discover that your denied grief does not overwhelm you. In the presence of unconditional love, you will discover that you can allow these feelings to be experienced but still survive them.

As you do your work, you will begin to experience the rewards of being in touch with your authentic feelings. You will begin to recognize the benefits of embarking on this journey and start to glimpse enhanced feelings of aliveness, curiosity and spontaneity.

The beauty of this is that when your carried pain is responded to in a hospitable way, you will no longer be controlled by it. To integrate your grief is to be able to listen to the music of the past while you begin to dance into the future.

Need 3: Developing a new self-identity

Your personal identity, or self-perception, is the result of the ongoing process of establishing a sense of who you are. I daresay that all of the losses revealed by your Carried Grief Self-Inventory and your work with your compassionate companion will have an impact on your self-identity.

When someone with whom you have had a relationship dies, for example, your self-identity, or the way you see yourself, naturally changes. If a sibling died, you may have gone from being a brother or sister to an "only child." The way you define yourself and the way society defines you is changed.

Other life losses may also have powerful impacts on your self-identity. If you have gone through a divorce, your self-identity may now include feelings of being unlovable. If you have or have had cancer, your self-identify may include feelings of bodily betrayal or being unfairly burdened or victimized.

Your compassionate companion will help you understand how your self-identity has been impacted by your life losses and carried grief. In acknowledging some painful aspects of your changed self-identity, you may release them. For example, some people who have knowingly or unknowingly seen themselves as victims go on to release their feelings of victimization and embrace more empowering concepts of self-identity.

Many catch-up mourners discover that as they work on this need, they ultimately discover some positive aspects of their changed self-identities. They often develop a renewed confidence in themselves and a more caring, kind and sensitive self-image.

Need 4: Searching for meaning

As you embrace the life losses that have resulted in your carried grief, you will naturally question the meaning and purpose of your life. Your compassionate companion will help you through this questioning process.

You will explore religious and spiritual values as you work on this need, and you may discover yourself asking "how" and "why" questions. Why did this happen to me? Why do people have to suffer? How could God let this happen?

Even though there are not always answers to these difficult questions, you will ultimately find value—and even peace—in wrestling with them. The process of searching for meaning in loss is lifelong. Like grief, it does not ever truly end. But you can achieve a peace in your search that allows you to live and love fully, to step out of the shadow of the ghosts of grief and into the light.

Need 5: Receiving ongoing support from others

I've already explained the need for a compassionate companion in reconciling your carried grief. You will also need the ongoing support of others in your life to move forward in wholeness. I encourage you to involve those you love in your struggles with reconciling your carried grief. Those closest to you deserve your honesty and you, in turn, deserve their support.

Opening up to your significant other, your children, your parents and your best friends about your awakening will help them understand the transformation you are experiencing. It will also help them embrace the new you that you are becoming.

In addition to your chosen compassionate companion, you may also want to seek ongoing support from a support group, a spiritual leader or others. You, in turn, may offer your support to someone else who is struggling with similar carried pain issues.

Step 4: Integrating Your Carried Grief

"Living is a constant process of deciding what we are going to do."
— Jose Ortega Gasset

When you have given attention to your carried grief in ways that it deserves and demands, you will begin to experience a sense of wholeness. To heal in grief literally means "to become whole." The key to integration of your grief is to make connections and keep making them as you learn to continue your changed life with fullness and meaning. While you have been shaped by your past experiences of carried grief, you can now become free in ways that give testimony to how you no longer need to be defined by it. Yes, the truth will set you free.

Obviously, to experience a new and changed wholeness requires that you engage actively in the work of mourning. It doesn't happen to you; you must stay open to that which has broken you. Even when you don't know exactly what lies ahead, you can learn to trust the process and open your heart to the healing that awaits you.

You may have been anchored for a long time in your fear and carried grief. But now you can begin to live authentically and be honest with yourself and those around you. As your new life unfolds, you will reconnect with parts of yourself that have been left behind and discover your new self. You can start having more fun and relax into the joy of being alive. Life broadens. You have longed to be free and now you realize you are. You have accepted responsibility for your healing.

Healing is a holistic concept that embraces the physical, emotional, cognitive, social and spiritual realms. Note that healing is not the same as curing, which is a medical term that means "remedying" or "correcting." You cannot remedy your carried pain, but you can reconcile it. You cannot correct carried grief, but you can heal it.

Reconciliation is a term I find more appropriate for what occurs as you participate in the catch-up mourning of carried grief. With reconciliation comes new life energy and the capacity to be optimistic about your life journey and to engage in the activities of being fully alive.

Reconciliation allows you to relax into the world around you and bathe yourself in gratitude. Reconciliation is not about "closure" but about "opening": opening further; learning more; connecting with the depths of your life losses; and becoming a more loving, kind and compassionate person. Instead of being among the living dead, you are awake, alive and hope-filled.

The Beauty of Now

Now you can be present to the beauty that surrounds you. Now you can be self-compassionate and experience the capacity to have joy in your life. Now you have gratitude that you entered into the wilderness of your grief. Now you are so thankful to have the capacity to give and receive love with an open heart. Now you are grateful that the meaning of life is found in living fully in the moment and not being bound by your past!

Part Five

Stepping into the light

" *Attending to our unattended*
sorrow opens the way to new life."
— Stephen Levine

Genuine healing means coming in tune with the truth; it means integrating pain into your heart and making peace with yourself and the world around you. You give attention to the carried grief of life losses and give voice to it.

So, healing involves...
...encountering what is most feared.
...opening to what it might be tempting
    to close yourself off from.
...a never-ending journey into wholeness.
...an honoring of your past as you
    hope for your future.
...a transformation of heart and soul.

Yes, healing from the carried pains of life losses requires that we surrender to the energies of grief and descend into and through the experience. Our carried pain has us living in the shadow of the ghosts of grief, and to heal our pain, we must first plunge deeper into the shadows before we can step into the light. In so doing, we create conditions that allow and encourage something new to arise from within us. With loving, compassionate companions, you can and will rise from the depths of your grief and discover unexpected healing and transformation. My hope is that in reading this book you have affirmed that this healing occurs not by separating yourself from pain but by attending to it.

Transformation literally means an entire change in form. Many catch-up mourners I have worked with have said to me, "I am a totally different person than I was before." Like them, you too can and will be different. Many have taught me that they have grown in their wisdom, in their gratitude, and in their compassion. My prayer for you is that you can also experience these kinds of transformations.

Discovering Your New Life

"Your life changes the moment you make a
new, congruent, and committed decision."
— Anthony Robbins

Congruency is a term used in geometry. Congruent triangles coincide at all points when superimposed upon each other. This is a state of being in agreement, a state of corresponding.

Years ago, psychologist Carl Rogers created a model of human behavior based on the concept of congruency. He believed that to fulfill our purpose as human beings, we need to be congruent on three levels. The core level, our essence, needs to be congruent with our middle level, which is what we perceive ourselves to be. The surface level, our "form," consists of our behaviors and the self we display to the outside world. To be congruent, what we do and how we act on the surface level needs to match how we perceive ourselves and what is in our essence.

If you are living congruently, you:

- try to be honest at all times.

- are aware of who you really are and do not wear masks.

- honestly claim your thoughts and speak them.

- honestly claim your feelings and show them.

- honestly claim your mistakes and try to correct them.

- honestly claim your doubts and questions and raise them.

- honestly claim your beliefs and live them.

If you are living congruently, you are the genuine article. Congruence is about living from the inside out, being aware of your essence and living it. As the saying goes, what you see is what you get. In my experience companioning thousands of people in grief, I have discovered that when we mourn authentically, we live more authentically from the inside out!

More of So Much More

*"He who has not looked on
sorrow will never see joy."*
— Kahlil Gibran

While going inside yourself to mourn your carried
grief and discover yourself is difficult, it is well
worth it. Mourning life losses and being congruent
with yourself and others can result in:

- More Meaning and Purpose
  We all hunger for meaning and purpose in our
  lives. However, if we carry the pain of grief, our
  numbness will mask this hunger.

  As you find safe people with whom to mourn
  your life losses, your conscious mourning will
  invite questions like, "Who am I?" and "What
  am I meant to do with my life?" "Does my life
  really matter?" Mourning life losses puts you
  face-to-face with the big questions of life.

  Befriending life losses seems to make us crave
  meaning and purpose in our everyday actions.
  Meaning is defined by intention and significance

and is the very opposite of just going through the motions of living. Giving attention to your life losses has a way of transforming your assumptions, values and priorities. You may now value material goods and status less and relationships more.

In a very real sense, mourning sets you on a path of searching your soul. Then the question becomes, where do you look to discover yourself? Paradoxically, as you mourn your life losses outwardly, you begin to look inside. Purpose is already within us, just waiting to be discovered.

If you open yourself to what is inside, you will find it. Once you have discovered it, you will be invited to live it.

To go inside and explore your life purpose can be a frightening experience. After all, the journey inside is risky. You might feel lost and alone. You might worry that you will have to make some significant life changes. In part, purpose means living inside the question, "How can I discover my purpose for being in this world and fulfill it?" Beyond that, it means being able to be a vital part of the universe and to be in harmony with something larger than yourself.

Softening to your carried pain often invites you to utilize your potential. In many ways, mourning your life losses seems to free the potential within to discover your gifts and put them to use in the world. Carried grief mutes your gifts, but now you can become free to make use of them. Helping others in some way, shape or form is, for many people who integrate loss into their lives, a vital part of discovering gifts and putting them to use. So ask yourself, how can I help my fellow human beings?

None of us wants to go through life dazed and numb, yet that is what we often do when we carry grief. When you mourn life losses and live congruently, you can discover a new sense of direction and purpose in everything you do. Purpose helps define our contribution to life. It may find expression through relationships, family, community, work, and spiritual concerns and acts. You may also become aware that you are fulfilling your destiny. And I ask you, what could be better than that?

- More Energy and Life Force
  Carried grief diminishes your awareness of what is going on around you. It's as if the lights are on, but nobody's home. It is like living in a fog and not being connected to yourself or others. Carried grief prevents you from being present in the immediacy of the moment. Reconciling your carried grief, on the other hand, allows you to notice things, both inside and out, that you have missed before.

Carried grief robs you of your energy and vitality. As you open to your mourning, you unleash your inner power and divine spark—that which gives depth and purpose to your living. When you experience the renewal of your divine spark, you have more energy and enthusiasm for living. Not only do you have greater stamina, you express vitality. You radiate positive energy and engage in life in ways that connect you to the greater world of humanity.

Life is the basic force that animates us. When you mourn and live congruently, it is as if you can wake up to life and experience more of it. Your senses become more acute and you become more open and engaged in what is going on around you. Rather than feeling numb and dazed, you feel alive, vibrant and vital.

Now you can engage fully in life. Instead of life just happening to you, now you understand more and your enhanced awareness unleashes energy to create your own destiny. Now you are not just existing, you are living abundantly.

- More Feelings
When you step out of the shadows of the ghosts of grief, you can experience your feelings more openly, honestly and deeply. You are able to feel a full range of emotions, from sadness, protest and anxiety to love, joy and passion. You become more authentic and alive.

As emphasized throughout this book, carried grief numbs your feelings and disengages you from life. This disengagement can result in a lack of awareness of not only your own feelings, but other people's feelings as well.

When you have masked feelings, you live with a false self—a life out of touch with feelings that can guide you. By contrast, when you become more conscious of your feelings, you begin to honor them and trust them. Learning to befriend your feelings allows you to become more expressive of your real self. The happy consequence is greater intimacy with yourself and others. Now, instead of being "checked-out," you are "checked-in!"

- More Love, Intimacy and Connection
  In becoming your congruent self, you come to know yourself more fully and others come to know you as well. Whereas carried grief closed your love down, you have now opened yourself up. Now you can allow yourself to be vulnerable and allow love in.

Mourning well results in loving well. You become a person you respect and value. Experiencing self-love allows you to receive the love you now open your heart to. You make yourself available and emanate a desire to connect deeply and intimately to those around you.

In opening your broken heart, you open yourself to the rebirth of living and loving until you die. We all need love in our lives. We seek love after mourning life losses because we come to realize love is the only thing we can't live without. In every breath you take, you can and will come to know this truth. No matter what else you pursue in life, love is always your most passionate and important quest. Love is the substance and essence of life. Opening your heart wide allows you to recognize that love is the foundation of your new life of passion and true joy.

You open yourself to meaningful, magical, soulful connections to others. There is no experience in life that can match the joy of giving and receiving love—and now you can travel on that path. A soulful love awaits you and now you have the energy and desire to experience it. Now you can have more life, more meaning and more love than you ever imagined possible.

• More Possibilities

Now life opens you up to a multitude of options. You may well discover an inner calling that invites you to follow your dreams. What have you always wanted to do but never did? What have you always told yourself was impossible? All that seemed impossible is now possible.

• More Quality of Experience

Your everyday activities become more purposeful as you achieve reconciliation of your carried grief. You understand more about why you do what you do each moment of your life. You feel deeper meaning in your living and have increased insight into why you think and feel the way you do.

• More Satisfaction and Fulfillment

Stepping out of the shadow of the ghosts of grief allows you to discover your talents and gifts. By developing yourself and embracing your gifts, you feel fulfilled and one with the world around you. As you project a spiritual optimism into the world, you experience true satisfaction in living your life.

- More Creativity
  Your unique talents are now released into the universe. You can now manifest your creativity and allow it to flourish. Your problem-solving and imaginative capacity increase.

- More Faith and Spirituality
  By slowing down and seeing deeper connections, you feel gratitude for what you have in life. You appreciate all that you have been given. The heart of faith is believing you are never alone. And now you realize you are not alone. You can see that life is a sacred journey and come to trust in the goodness that surrounds you.

You may well discover that you have the opportunity to become what could be called a "spiritual gourmet." While a food gourmet knows how to put together a wonderful menu, a spiritual gourmet knows how to put together a wonderful life. You can harmoniously meld life ingredients such as work, play and service—all surrounded in love.

- More Truth

  Making peace with your pain invites you to live the truth. Living the truth is itself a journey into self-reflection and discovery. To live in truth is to be conscious that your truth may not be now what it once was or what it will be in the future, but it is your obligation to live and speak your truth in the present moment. Authentic mourning encourages you to search for the truth inside you that has been longing to be expressed and to find the words to speak it. Surrender yourself to the truth, for to live your life in truth is to live in freedom from the pain that muted your spirit.

Touching the World Around You

"If you have anything really valuable to contribute to the world, it will come through the expression of your own personality, that single spark of divinity that sets you off and makes you different from every other living creature."
— Bruce Barton

Perhaps most importantly, as your individual transformation evolves, you become capable of giving yourself to something larger. We all have something to contribute to the larger world, a unique gift or vision. And in your renewed capacity to reach out and connect, you discover your wholeness. This is the essence of healing from the carried grief of life losses. Now you experience compassion and balance.

You may even go in search of other fellow strugglers who have carried grief and reach out to them from a place of compassion. Together you can come to acknowledge that healing and transformation go beyond a spiritual detour of the suffering that accompanies life losses. Now you can live your life deeply and fully, not only healing yourself, but compassionately reaching out and engaging in the world around you. In doing so, you are a stimulus for healing energy and global healing. Thank you for joining me on this journey!

Living on Purpose and Making a Difference in the World

"Life is a promise; fulfill it."
— Mother Teresa

Living on purpose provides you with a sense of direction. Without meaning and purpose, you may have lost your way and lived in the shadow of the ghosts of grief. My hope is that this book serves as a life compass that not only gives you direction but imbues everything you do with purpose.

Until you make peace with your purpose, you will never discover joy in your life. The key to living on purpose is to bring together the needs of the world around you with your unique gifts in an effort to discover your calling. Your calling is your inner voice reminding you of your God-given gifts and challenging you to use them. Your calling allows you to contribute actively to the world.

Joy will come to you when you know in your heart that what you are doing matters. Joy will happen when you see your life as making a real difference.

To discover your calling requires spending enough time with your soul to know just what it is you are called to be and do. And out of this awareness you can live out your calling.

I truly believe that at the end of life, there are five questions that really matter:

1. Have I given love well?
2. Have I received love well?
3. Have I mourned life losses well?
4. Have I contributed to making the world a better place?
5. Have I lived an on-purpose life?

Living on purpose can be a way of life, a discipline to be practiced every day. It mandates a real desire to face each new day with the question, "Why did I get out of bed this morning?" The good sense to ask and the boldness to answer this critical question forms the centerpiece of living on purpose.

So mourn your life losses, live congruently and discover your purpose and calling. Without a doubt, the most fortunate people in the world are those who live each day from a place of meaning and purpose. Their sense of meaning and purpose inspires them to fill their lives with growth, challenges, passion and love!

Carrying Your Transformation Forward

> *"The future enters into us, in order to transform itself in us, long before it happens."*
> — Rainer Maria Rilke

Tomorrow is now. It is here. It is waiting for you. You have many choices in living the transformation that healing your carried pain will bring to your life. Be open to the direction your life is now taking you. Listen to the wisdom of your inner voice and follow the guidance of your inner spirit. Make choices that are congruent with what you have learned on your journey.

Look for the graces that surround you. Remember that grace expands your intellect by gifting you with intuitive wisdom. You can now be guided by something you would not find through logic. Now you can find your true life path, live through the pain of life losses, and extend unconditional love.

What are some of the signs that you are now living free of your carried grief, that you have stepped out of the shadow of the ghosts of grief and into the light?

- You feel a sense of belonging in the world around you, as if the universe was embracing you.

- You experience a full sense of joy, of not being alone as you face things in life.

- You experience times when you feel you are in contact with the source of wisdom, love and healing.

- You notice a persistent sense that someone or something genuinely wants you to evolve and fulfill your potential. This comforting presence is supporting you without judgments or conditions.

- You feel mysteriously supported and loved at times when you need it, keeping you open to the divine. You discover that giving love is ever more vital than getting love.

- You persevere even in the face of adversity. You create goals for yourself and set about accomplishing them with continued, patient effort. You can choose to work, not just when it is required. You seek self-discipline and self-responsibility.

- You experience a loving presence in the universe that surrounds you. You can experience the feeling of being personally loved by the people in your life and you can express love to them.

- You experience a gentleness of spirit and kindness of heart. Gentleness eases the way and adds grace to your life. It softens your sorrows and cushions the burdens. Kindness becomes a natural virtue you express in the world. Your kindness soothes, calms, and renews you and those your life touches. Kindness adds a hope-filled texture to every aspect of your life.

- You experience the beauty around you. You come to realize that this moment, this day, this relationship, and this life are all unique, exquisite, and unrepeatable. There will be no moment exactly like this one. There will be no other day that unfolds precisely the events and experiences of this day. You can now embrace every moment. You now have gratitude that your entire life can now be found in the timelessness of the moment you are in—right now.

- You experience gratitude for being more alive than you were in the past. You are aware your emotional and spiritual healing has transformed you and resulted in new energy in your body, nourishment in your mind, and illumination in your soul.

My Prayer For You

May you be free from your carried grief and discover the freedom to live life with purpose and meaning every moment of each day. May you step out of the shadow of the ghosts of grief and turn your face to the radiance of joy. May you live in the continued awareness that you are being cradled in love by a caring presence that never deserts you. May you keep your heart open wide and be receptive to what life brings you, both happy and sad. And, in doing so, may you create a pathway to living your life fully and on purpose until you die.

Manufactured by Amazon.ca
Bolton, ON